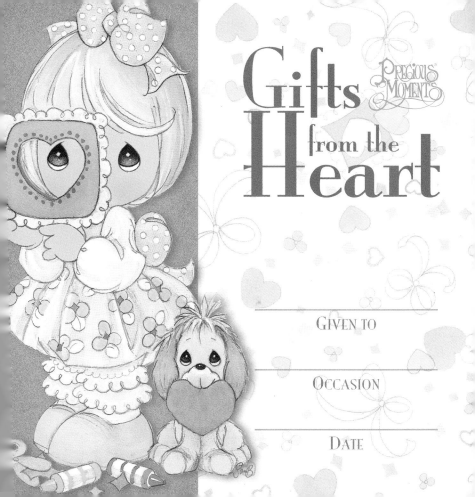

Gifts

PRECIOUS MOMENTS

from the Heart

GIVEN TO

OCCASION

DATE

"And now abide faith, hope, love, these three;
but the greatest of these is love."

1 Corinthians 13:13

Unlike anything else in His creation, God created people not only with the capacity to love, but with the necessity to give and receive it. The one who selected this special Scripture book for you is communicating his or her heart through this gift. In these beautiful pages of heart-warming illustrations and encouraging Scriptures, you'll see a glimpse of someone else's love for you, too — your heavenly Father's. As you delight in the familiar faces of Sam Butcher's adorable characters, see yourself in the same light of innocence and affection that God sees you. Then memorize the simple verses, so that even in your darkest days, you'll remember the love of God, friends, and family you discovered here.

You shall love the LORD
your God with all your heart,
with all your soul,
and with all your strength.

Deuteronomy 6:5

Love does no harm
to a neighbor;
therefore love is the
fulfillment of the law.

Romans 13:10

For all the law is
fulfilled in one word,
even in this:
"You shall love your
neighbor as yourself."

Galatians 5:14

And let us consider
one another in order
to stir up love
and good works.

Hebrews 10:24

Beloved,
if God so loved us,
we also ought to love
one another.

1 John 4:11

For we have great joy
and consolation in your love,
because the hearts of
the saints have been
refreshed by you.

Philemon 7

This is My commandment, that you love one another as I have loved you.

John 15:12

By this all will know
that you are My disciples,
if you have love for
one another.

John 13:35

My little children,
let us not love in
word or in tongue,
but in deed and in truth.

1 John 3:18

And may the Lord
make you increase
and abound in love to
one another and to all,
just as we do to you.

1 Thessalonians 3:12

Be kindly affectionate
to one another with
brotherly love, in honor
giving preference
to one another.

Romans 12:10

Love suffers long
and is kind;
love does not envy;
love does not parade itself,
is not puffed up.

1 Corinthians 13:4

And now abide faith,
hope, love, these three;
but the greatest of
these is love.

1 Corinthians 13:13

> "If we love one another, God abides in us,
> and His love has been perfected in us."
>
> 1 John 4:12

Surely the Word of God and these encouraging illustrations have touched your heart and released your spirit to rejoice in God's unchanging love for you. As your cup overflows with His goodness, now is the time to notice those around you whose vessels are dry, empty, and in need of the sweet refreshment you yourself have just received. May God's grace go with you as you take these words of love deep into your soul, and pour them out in showers of blessings to others that God brings across your path. Remember that as you give of what has been given to you in a word of encouragement, a hug, or a gift, the Lord Himself will replenish you, increasing your capacity to receive and revel in His love.

Walk in love,
as Christ also has loved us
and given Himself for us,
an offering and a
sacrifice to God for a
sweet-smelling aroma.

Ephesians 5:2